ANIMALS AT THE ZOO: FUN ANIMALS WE LOVE

Zoos around the world
are trying to coordinate
efforts to breed
endangered species.

The giraffe is is the tallest land animal in the world. Fully grown giraffes stand 5-6 meters tall. The males are taller than females.

Giraffes use their height to browse on leaves and buds in treetops that few other animals can reach.

The koala is a
tree-dwelling
marsupial
mammal. Koalas
are native to
Australia. They
can only be found
in the eucalyptus
forests.

The word "koala"
means "no drink"
and it refers to
their ability to go
for many days
without water.

Penguins are
a group of
aquatic, flightless
birds living in
the Southern
Hemisphere.
Penguins have
adapted flippers
to help them swim
in the water.

Penguins have excellent hearing and rely on distinct calls to identify their mates when returning to the crowded breeding grounds.

Peafowl belong to pheasant
family. Male peafowl
is called peacock while
female is called peahen.

Peacocks are known for their amazing eye-spotted tail feathers. It is is believed to be a way to attract females for mating purposes.

Elephants are the largest land-living mammal in the world. They live in Asia and Africa. Adult elephants weigh between 5,000 and 14,000 pounds.

Elephants spend 16 hours a day eating. They eat grass, leaves, shrubs, branches and fruits.

Red panda is a close
relative of giant panda.
They are also known as
'fire fox' because of
its red color of the fur.

Red Pandas spend most of
their time in trees. They
live in Sichuan and Yunnan
provinces of China, Himalayas,
Myanmar and Nepal.

When a zebra is attacked other members of it's herd will form a circle and face the predator to help the attacked zebra.